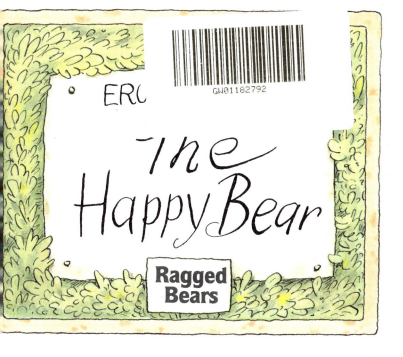

ERO

The
Happy Bear

Ragged
Bears

The little bear spends happy hours
wading through a sea of flowers.

Our friend the bear has come to see
the owl inside his hollow tree.

Frog and bear sit in the car.
I don't think they will travel far.

In the rain butt sleeps the bear.
The sun's too hot, with all that hair.

Here come the rain and stormy blast –
the little bear runs home quite fast.

The hedgehog blows the tuba,
the bear plays on the flute,
but though he loves the music,
the toad can't sing a note.

The grey wolf has a wicked grin.
The bear will never let him in.

The flying carpet is the mouse's.
The bear likes flying above the houses.

The bear has found some honey here,
but all the bees have found the bear.

Often, as the sun goes down,
the bear and ravens sail around.

The bear is giving a fireside chat,
telling his stories to the cats.

The autumn leaves fall from the trees,
the bear is smiling in his dreams.

The water's frozen, far and near.
Now bear is happy in his fur.

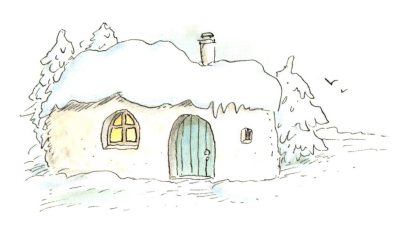

Tobogganing is splendid fun!
Bear and hedgehog take a run.

Originally published as DAS SCHÖNE BÄRENLEBEN
© 1990 Beltz Verlag, Weinheim and Basel
Programm Beltz & Gelberg, Weinheim. All rights reserved
English edition first published by
Ragged Bears Ltd, Ragged Appleshaw, Andover,
Hampshire SP11 9HX
Translated by Patricia Crampton
Translation © 1990 Ragged Bears Ltd
Printed in West Germany
ISBN 1 870817 48 6

If you have enjoyed this book, be sure to have:

A BED FOR THE MOUSE
FRIENDS FOR THE BEAR
BIRDS, BATS, MICE AND CATS

also published by Ragged Bears Ltd

The LITTLEST BOOKS Collection from Ragged Bears

The Littlest Book of Kittens
The Littlest Book for a Friend
The Littlest Book Just for You
The Littlest Book of the Heart
The Littlest Book of Birds
The Littlest Christmas Book
The Littlest Book for Mother's Day
The Littlest Easter Bunny Book
The Littlest Book of Bears
The Littlest Book of Trees
The Littlest Book of Cats and Mice
The Littlest Book of Small Things
The Littlest Book for Every Day
The Littlest Book of the Way
The Littlest Book for a Joyful Event